T0078076

Dear Zoe and Halle

Life advice from a mother
to her daughters

Noelle Tredt

BALBOA.PRESS
A DIVISION OF HAY HOUSE

Balboa Press books may be ordered through booksellers or by contacting:

Balboa Press
A Division of Hay House
1663 Liberty Drive
Bloomington, IN 47403
www.balboapress.com
844-682-1282

Because of the dynamic nature of the Internet, any web addresses or
links contained in this book may have changed since publication and
may no longer be valid. The views expressed in this work are solely those
of the author and do not necessarily reflect the views of the publisher,
and the publisher hereby disclaims any responsibility for them.

The author of this book does not dispense medical advice or prescribe
the use of any technique as a form of treatment for physical, emotional,
or medical problems without the advice of a physician, either directly
or indirectly. The intent of the author is only to offer information
of a general nature to help you in your quest for emotional and
spiritual well-being. In the event you use any of the information in
this book for yourself, which is your constitutional right, the author
and the publisher assume no responsibility for your actions.

Any people depicted in stock imagery provided by Getty Images are
models, and such images are being used for illustrative purposes only.
Certain stock imagery © Getty Images.

Print information available on the last page.

ISBN: 978-1-9822-6842-8 (sc)
ISBN: 978-1-9822-6843-5 (e)

Balboa Press rev. date: 05/20/2021

Contents

Foreword

S YOU BOTH know, my grandfather died very suddenly at age 52, then my mom also died when she was 52. As I'm writing this, I am 51, and will turn 52 in 2 months. Honestly—I do NOT think I'm going to die when I'm 52. I think I will live well into my 80's, maybe even 90's, healthy and happy. Then just go to bed one night and wake up dead. That's what I think is actually going to happen. But with the big 5-2 approaching, it did get me thinking of all the things that I still have to teach you. All of the wisdom that I still have, and that I'd love to pass along to you. It just seems that life gives opportunities for your "elders" to pass along the good stuff to the younger generations. And if for some reason I were not here for those opportunities.....well, I certainly wouldn't want you girls to miss out!

So first let me just say that if I do pass over to the next phase, I realize it will really suck for you guys. But please know that it will not suck for me. As I look back at my 51 and 5/6 years on this earth, I am amazed, humbled, and astounded by how truly good my life has been. I was raised by people who loved me deeply, and I in turn have loved others deeply. I'm going to try to sum up a few things in my life, with highlights, just to remind you of some history of your mama....

I was born Dec. 16th, 1967, in Missoula, Montana, to Patricia and Rod Kulstad. I joined my 14 month old sister, Nicole. We lived outside of Missoula, in Gold Creek, for a couple of years, moved into Missoula, then East Helena, then to Helena before I was 3. We then moved to Stevensville, to be closer to Grama and Grampa Kulstad. Rod and Kate were still alive when you guys were born. They were my dad's parents, and they were a huge part of my childhood. When living in Stevensville, while Nicole was in kindergarten, mom and dad divorced. So Mom, Nicole and I then moved to Anaconda, where mom was raised, to be closer to my other Grama—Ruby. This was mom's mom. Mom's dad—Hap—was the grampa that died at age 52, of a very sudden heart attack, several years before I was born—before Pat and Rod got married. But anyway, Mom, Nicole and I lived in Anaconda until I was in 2nd grade and Nicole in 3rd. Mom had met Jim Skelton, who became my stepdad in 1976. Once mom and Jim were married, we moved to Sunburst, Montana for a short time (6 months), then to Cut Bank, where I eventually graduated high school in 1986.

After graduation, I first went to the University of Montana in Missoula for 3 years, then transferred to Western Washington University in Bellingham, Washington in 1989. I graduated there in 1992, then went to PT school at Pacific University in Forest Grove, Oregon, graduating as a physical therapist in 1995. I moved to Memphis for my first job, was there for about 5 months, then transferred to the VA hospital in Nashville, Tennessee. I worked there for 2 years, then Grama Pat died at the age of 52. It was through that experience that your dad and I became a couple. We had been friends since college—about 11 years. But going back to Montana to take care of things after mom died, was when your dad and I went from friends to a couple. I moved back to Montana in 1997, and we got engaged in 1998. Dad and I were married July 18, 1998 at Holland Lake Lodge in the Seeley-Swan Valley of Montana. We were both 30 years old.

We lived in Corvallis, Montana, where dad owned a Farmer's Insurance Agency in Hamilton and I worked at Marcus Daly Hospital. Zoe was born there Oct 4, 1999 and Halle on Feb 17, 2001. Soon after Halle was born, we decided to try a new place...a new state, and headed to Wyoming (Halle was about 6 months old and Zoe was 2). We lived in Sheridan, Wyoming for a bit, then permanently moved to Buffalo at Christmas of 2002. We lived out on Redwood Ave, 3 miles west of town, until you guys were in school. Then the 3 of us moved to Sheridan for a bit, where Zoe went to first and second grade, and Halle went to kindergarten and first grade. We moved back to Buffalo to the house on High Street, where you started third and second grades. We lived there until taking off for our year of travel in the 5th wheel. We had planned on returning, but ended up settling in Highmore, South Dakota in time for Zoe to start 7th grade and Halle to start 6th grade. This became our home until you guys graduated. I know you both know a lot of this, but It's good to get it onto paper and make sure you know our early history. From there……I think you know how things went, and if you need a boost to the memories, you have plenty of scrapbooks to remind you of your early lives. But amongst all of these facts—the nuts and bolts of our history—I want to also let you know that my life was so much more than just that. As I said when I started this whole history lesson—I had an amazing life. Here are some of the highlights….

I've been on a couple of cruises—to Mexico and the Caribbean. I've swam with and fed sting rays. I've camped on a beach, in a tent, in Mexico. I've been rock climbing (with a guy named Cliff 😊). I've snow skied, water skied, and jet skied. I've been on a sailboat, and helped friends race that boat, and spent the night gently rocking on that boat. I woke up on my 23rd birthday, on a train in the Swiss Alps, with big snowflakes quietly floating down. I've been to Hawaii, floated in a quiet glider over the coast, and snorkeled amongst the coral. I've seen the Pope speak, at Vatican City, in Rome. I took stained glass art classes and made several stained-glass projects. I've jumped off a cliff into Lake Powell, Arizona. I've been to several pro football games, a pro basketball game, and pro baseball games. I've snowmobiled in Yellowstone Park, and had a herd of buffalo pass so closely I could have reached out and touched them. I worked for really rich people in New York City, and went to Broadway plays, and Central Park, and Coney Island. I hiked with friends in the northern Cascade Mountains, with backpacks, and spent the night in a tent by a stream. I went parasailing in the Bahamas. I've been clam diving, charter boat fishing, and crabbing.

I've been to Mexico, Canada, the Cayman Islands, Jamaica, the Bahamas, the Netherlands, Belgium, Luxembourg, France, Germany, Switzerland, and Italy. Not to mention all over the United States. And as you both know, we had the most amazing year traveling and living in a 5th wheel camper. We ate Fondue in Nashville, took a fancy brunch cruise out of Daytona Beach, Florida, went fishing in the Keys, kayaked on the Estero River and saw a manatee, watched dolphins at sunrise in St. Augustine. We went to a spring baseball game between the Cardinals and Red Sox, and saw Eric Church in concert. We went to New York City twice—once in the camper and once to visit the Wages in Brooklyn. We saw all of the lit up monuments at night in Washington D.C. We ate at a Mexican restaurant for Easter in South Carolina, and went fishing for catfish on Lake Greenwood. We saw the sights in Charleston, South Carolina and Savannah, Georgia. We took a brunch sail on an old sailboat in the Boston Harbor, and took a duck tour of Boston on a vehicle that was both a tour bus and a tour boat. We saw Plymouth rock, ate a bunch of clam chowder, and spent a weekend in Nantucket.

Oh. My. Goodness. I really could go on and on, and list several more pages of amazing things I've done in my lifetime. But I think you get the point. If I were to pass over, and leave this earthly life behind…..believe me. I have absolutely no regrets. I have lived a full, fulfilling, amazing life!!!

Now…..on to the real reason for this long letter. Or short book. Or whatever it turns out to be. I'm going to bless you with the wisdom that I have gained, through trial and error, here on this earth. (You lucky girls…)

Chapter 1

It's All About Your Perspective

*W*E CANNOT CHANGE our pasts. The past is the past; what happened happened, and arguing with your past—wishing it was different than how it was—can bring you so much unhappiness. But our perspective....how we think about our pasts....is ENTIRELY up to us.

No matter how "bad" the situation seems, it can be altered purely due to our perspective. We can choose to get the lessons from the situation, see the silver lining, and then move on. We do not have to look back at things in our past with regret. The relationship that broke your heart, the job you wanted so badly but didn't get, the loss of loved ones in your life. Those things will happen. And there are those who allow those circumstances to scar them, and make them shrink, and make them build walls around their hearts. But that is a choice. Those

1

circumstances do not have to break you. And it sounds like a cliché, but those circumstances truly can make you stronger.

You are going to screw up. You are going to fail. You are going to say the wrong things, and do the wrong things, and act the wrong way. And at times, people you love are going to screw up. They are going to say and do mean and hurtful things. And life on this earth is going to seem screwed up. Crappy circumstances and events will happen. BUT....and this is an awfully LARGE BUT....but—that's OK. That is just a little sliver of life. The quote/unquote bad stuff is just part of the deal. And I don't know why so many people just hang on to that bad stuff, and give it so much more importance than it deserves. Because at the other end of the spectrum is the amazing stuff. You are going to excel. You are going to say the right things, and do the right things, and a lot in life is going to turn out beautifully. And people you love are going to say incredible things, and do fantastic things that will make your heart sing. And wonderful and amazing circumstances and events will happen. That's the stuff we want to focus on. That's the stuff we want to give all of the importance to.

And then, of course, is a whole lot of the medium stuff. The day to day, very routine, run-of-the-mill, ordinary stuff that makes up a big chunk of life here on earth. This is where perspective is so important. If you can look at all of this routine stuff in a way that is positive, and find contentment in it, that is one of those keys to happiness. To be so thankful for the blah, blah, blah parts of life. To really appreciate the small stuff.

As you move through life, and have more and more memories racking up, this will form "your past". And if you can look back at your past with rose colored glasses, and see that it all worked out the way it was supposed to work out, well—that's an amazing way to look back at your life.

So I want you girls to really understand this. And put this into practice. I truly believe that my past happened EXACTLY HOW IT WAS SUPPOSED TO. I have peace with my past--mistakes and all. I have learned from my past. And I can honestly look back and see the beauty in my past, and be thankful for it—for ALL of it. My past has shaped me into the person that I am, and I happen to like who I am😊. You can't love who you are and not love the journey that made you.

Chapter 2

Your Thoughts Drive Everything

EVERY RESULT IN your life comes from you either taking action or not taking action. And the actions you have or have not taken have been driven by feelings and emotions inside of you. And all of those feelings and emotions come from one thing—your thoughts. Isn't that amazing? Read that again. My feelings, 100%, come from my thoughts. That, right there, is the secret sauce to life.

I lived a whole lot of my life just skipping right over the thought part. I really and truly thought that all of my feelings came from circumstances. From either events or other people. I thought that life was just happening TO me, and that caused me to feel a certain way. Had NO CLUE that it was not the circumstances—but my thoughts ABOUT the circumstances, that was actually making me have certain emotions.

My job is not stressing me out. My thoughts about my job are causing stress. That person is not causing me to be angry. My thoughts about that person and what he/she did are making me angry. My failure in the past is not causing me to feel unworthy. My thoughts about failing in the past are making me feel unworthy. And on the other side of the coin…happiness is not found outside of myself, either. Happiness is not found in a different job, a bigger bank account, a thinner body, or a better spouse. Emotions are all INTERNAL—they do not come from EXTERNAL sources.

And it all starts with my thoughts. And I don't know about you, but I LOVE THIS! I mean this gives me all the power in the world. I do not have to rely on anyone else, any circumstance, any OUTSIDE experience to create my happiness. I can choose to think positive thoughts and create my own happiness. That is amazing!

So often, circumstances happen to us in life, and they are completely out of our control. But we can choose to think about those circumstances ANY WAY WE WANT TO, and that will create our feelings about the experience. I think that is so cool.

Now, that is not to say that we have to choose positive emotions all the time. I mean, to really live life, we need to experience every emotion. So sometimes we are going to choose to be sad. And sometimes we will choose to be anxious, or angry, or frustrated, or whatever. But we need to OWN those emotions and truly realize that the emotion comes from our thoughts. Other people cannot make us feel a certain way—only our thoughts about what that person said or did can make us feel a certain way.

But I think it's important to fully experience emotions. Really be with that emotion and feel it. Feelings left unfelt will grow. Sadness can turn to grief. Anger can turn to rage. And doubt can turn into crippling fear. And I think really feeling our feelings will help us move through them, and come out on the other side. It is when we try to resist our feelings, when we try to avoid them, that we will eat too much. Or drink too much. Or shop too much. Or whatever too much. I think that addictions derive from us not wanting to feel our feelings.

It is also true that we need contrast in the world to really feel the good emotions. You know how you go through a sickness—like the flu or something. And when you finally feel good again, you feel really good. You realize that you kind of take for granted just being well and feeling good all the time. But it took the feeling crappy to really feel the feeling good. It takes sadness to really feel the happiness. It takes the stress to really feel the calm. It takes the fear to really feel the confidence.

So the lesson here, my sweet daughters, is that happiness really does come from inside. I know we've all seen that written on a bumper sticker, but it is so true. Living life to the fullest is feeling the full range of emotions, but they all can be felt inside a container of overall joy. And no matter the emotions you go through, you can always choose happiness. Right now. No matter what is going on in your life. And that is some powerful stuff.

Now, all of that being said, I do realize that controlling our thoughts is not always easy. Our human brains sometimes just go down these rabbit holes of negative thinking. But the first step is to just get aware. They say we have an average of 60,000 thoughts per day. So there's no way we can monitor all of our thoughts. But if we know that our thoughts create our feelings, then we can monitor THAT. If you tune in and realize that you are feeling sad, or anxious, or guilty, (or any other negative emotion), and then dig in a little deeper, and think about the thoughts—the sentences in your brain—that are causing the sadness or anxiety or guilt, well—that's the first step. You are now aware of your thoughts. It's kind of like just being the observer of the thoughts—not the one thinking.

When I was first learning to do this, I was in a really big hurry to identify those thoughts so that I could change them, as quickly as possible. So I wasn't giving myself time to process these thoughts and feelings. Therefore, they just kept coming back. I noticed patterns of thought that occurred over and over and over. Then I learned that second step. After becoming aware of the thoughts, then I just let them be for awhile. I became curious about my thoughts. I would realize that I was telling myself certain sentences in my brain, and I would be interested about where those thoughts came from, and what in my past maybe made me think that way. Then I just learned to make space for it all. To just be with the sadness, or the anxiety, or the guilt. I allowed myself to really feel what that emotion felt like. That's the second step, that I think is SO important. Because what that does, is make you realize that feeling your feelings is not going to hurt you. Yes, it is unpleasant to feel a negative emotion, but if you allow yourself to feel it, you realize that you CAN feel negative emotion, and get through it. Then you're not so apt to avoid it, or stuff it down, or resist it.

So now you've become aware of your thoughts, and allowed space for the emotions those thoughts are causing. Then and only then can you be ready for the third step. And that is to try to change the thoughts, even just a little bit, in the direction of a better feeling emotion. There's more to come on that in another chapter. But for now, I think if you can get these concepts, about your thoughts creating your feelings, that then drive your actions or inactions, that will get you the results in your life. Well, if you can get those concepts at a much younger age than I got them, you will have a serious leg up on your overall psychological health and emotional maturity.

Chapter 3

Spirituality

WE DID NOT raise you girls going to church regularly. There are a lot of reasons for that. I have had my struggles with formal religion. And God knows the journey I have been on during my life to find my purpose and see the big picture. But I have always believed strongly in God. Call it what you will, but I believe there is a Creator, a Source, a Higher Power. And these last few years I have really strengthened my relationship with God. I've prayed since I was a little girl. Grama Pat was raised Catholic. And although she eventually turned away from that religion, she taught us the Lord's Prayer, praying the rosary, and saying the Catholic grace before meals. I went through phases in my life where I just repeated written words to pray. I had phases where I just chatted with God, trying to talk to him like a friend and get him to talk back to me. I went through phases where I begged and pleaded with him, and where I questioned what the heck he was doing with us down here on earth. I even went through phases where I was really mad at him and purposefully turned away, or at least ignored him. Now I am going through a phase where I believe strongly in his "helpers." I believe in Angels, and departed loved ones, and Spirit Guides, who are all helping me. God has sent us helpers to guide us through this earthly existence. But here's the thing....I believe they cannot help us until we ASK them to help us. God gave us free will. And except for extreme life or death circumstances, I don't think our spiritual team can mess with that free will. So they can't help us until we ask for their help. I've been asking my team for all kinds of help lately—big and small—and am truly amazed at how they are right here helping me. I am praying regularly. And trusting. I truly believe God has only 3 answers to our prayers. 1. Yes. 2. Yes, but not right now. And 3. No....I have something much better planned for you. That's it. Those three answers are the only three answers there are. But that takes a lot of trust. A lot of faith. A lot of utter belief that things will turn out exactly the way they are supposed to turn out.

I can't imagine going through this earthly life not believing in God. Believing that this is all just some big accident. That we die and that's it. It's over. No...there is no way that I can believe that. I used to think that I was a human being and I HAD a soul. Now I believe I AM a soul—that is the real me--and I HAVE a body. My body is just the vehicle for getting around on this earth. But its not the real me. Not even my mind is the real me. My mind, or human brain, is just a bunch of neural circuits, full of memory and learning and patterns and thoughts and behaviors. But that's not even the real me. That Divine Light inside of me, that Inner Being in me that connects with Source—that is the real me. I am beginning to understand that we are just energy. EVERYTHING is just energy. And our earthly bodies are vibrating at a certain frequency. And when we pass over to the other side, our frequencies change. Angels have a much higher frequency of vibration. That's why we don't necessarily communicate with them the same way we communicate with others on earth. But I believe if we stay open, and really watch for the signs, our Angels are constantly communicating with us. And God is communicating with us. When we watch a sunset, with the vibrant oranges and pinks and yellows as the sun sinks below the horizon….God is communicating with us. And when we listen to music, or watch a ballerina, or study great works of art…God is communicating with us. When a baby is born, or a disease is cured, or a body heals after a surgery….God is communicating with us. We just have to stay awake, and keep our minds open.

And I am such a big believer in gratitude. Being grateful is another secret to life. I am in awe every single day of the goodness in my life. And I am so thankful for it. And I tell God every day how thankful I am. I really do count my blessings. This is one of my favorite tricks if I am having a bad day. In my mind, I go to the beginning of my day and start saying all the things I am thankful for. I am grateful for that big, comfy bed that I woke up in. And my ability to get up out of that bed with my healthy body. And coffee—oh so thankful for that first hot cup of

13

coffee. Then I get to hop into a hot shower. With clean water. And use good smelling shampoo and conditioner and soap. And I dry off with a fluffy towel….etc. I go through my whole day in my mind, and count every single blessing I can think of, and that bad day suddenly doesn't seem so bad after all.

This past year I have really gotten into meditation. I meditate almost every day. I usually do a guided meditation with an app or with a YouTube meditation. Then I do a 5 minute meditation where I just try to concentrate on my breathing. As my mind starts to wander, and it always does, I just notice the thought, let it float away, and bring my focus back to my breathing. This is a little exercise in mind training. And I love it. The more I do it, the more I am training my brain to focus on the here and now. They say that learning to live in the NOW is the secret to a happy life. And I believe that may be true. It seems we humans are so busy rehashing our past, or worrying about our future. Learning to focus on the here and now is just being mindful of this moment in time. Really focusing on this moment right now. We can sure let a lot of life slip right past us and not even notice it. I am really trying to live more mindful, and although it is challenging, it is pretty awesome☺.

But the point of this chapter, is to say that I hope you girls have some sense of spirituality. Maybe not formal religion—although maybe. I just want you both to realize that there is something bigger than all of us. A source of divine life that is right here, within us, at all times. And all we have to do is choose to connect with it. I wouldn't trade my journey of connecting with this source for all of the money in the world. Because that journey is still going on, and is leading me to a richer, more intimate relationship with God. And I wish for you both a lifetime journey of discovering God for yourselves.

Chapter 4

It All Starts With Loving Yourself

BELIEVE THAT EVERY experience in our life is really driven from what we think about ourselves. Loving myself starts with liking myself, which starts with respecting myself, which starts with saying nice things to myself in my head. This has been a long journey for me. And I have to admit that I have spent a lot of years hating myself. I have really struggled with self-esteem, poor self-worth, and even self-loathing at times. And the journey to change this came from awareness. Just being aware of the mean things I was saying to myself in my head. I really had no idea that I was doing this. It was quite the eye-opener to just become aware of my thoughts. Remember how I said that we can't monitor our 60,000 thoughts per day, so we have to monitor our feelings? I started to learn that when I was feeling crappy about myself, I needed to just stop and look at my thoughts. And I was pretty shocked at what I was saying to myself. I would NEVER say to another human being the things I was saying to me.

So I started to change it. I purposely started saying nicer things to myself. I made a habit of saying nice things every day. At first I tried to go straight for the absolute opposite thing that I had been thinking—straight up to the top of the scale. So for instance, if I stopped and noticed myself saying "Good Lord I am fat and disgusting." I would try to switch it to "I am beautiful." But I'll be honest, I didn't believe it, so it didn't really work. Then I learned to bridge my thoughts. I had to think things that I absolutely, 100% believed. So I would change "I am fat and disgusting" to "I have a nice smile with nice teeth." I believed that was absolutely true. Then I would think about the wonder of my body. The fact that I can walk, and that my heart beats all the time—whether I am awake or sound asleep. I thought of all the times I got a cut or scrape, and my amazing body healed it. Then I made friends with my arms. I switched my thoughts from "Gross. Look at these bingo wings." To "these arms allowed me to hold my sweet baby girls when they were infants." And I slowly made friends with all of my pieces parts. It was a process, to say the least. But basically, I just got more aware of my thoughts about myself, and I gradually changed them. And finally I got to "I am beautiful." And I 100% believed it. And it was amazing.

Because here is what I've learned. I have to have my own back. I have to be my own bestie. Because people will come into my life and people will pass out of my life. But I will have me for my lifetime and beyond.

And if I treat myself with kindness, and compassion, and understanding....then I will treat others with kindness, and compassion, and understanding. A good life starts with loving yourself. And I want you girls to get that. I don't want it to take you as long as it took me to get that. I want you to actively work on loving yourself. And again....it starts with liking yourself, which comes from respecting yourself, which starts with talking to yourself positively in your mind.

Chapter 5

Treating Others With Kindness

I WAS JUST A kid when my mom told me this one. She said that we really have no idea what another person is going through. That grumpy old man at the store may have lost his wife a few weeks ago. That lady that just cut us off in traffic may be thinking of her dog that just got put down. And that kid that is bullying that other kid may get smacked around regularly at home. We just have no idea what others are dealing with. So be kind. That doesn't mean we have to be doormats, or allow others to mistreat us. We have to stand up for ourselves and set healthy boundaries to protect ourselves. But in the back of your minds, always give people the benefit of the doubt, and be kind. You have no control over how others act, but you ALWAYS have control over the way YOU act.

People talk about the purpose of life. Well, this is what I believe. The purpose of life is to be happy and to be kind. That's it. If we continually work on happiness—even through the hardships and tough times and really crappy parts of life; if we continually try to see the good parts, and find the joy in living this earthly life; and just be good to others--be kind to them; then I believe we can live a life with purpose. Treat others with respect and compassion. That is really our purpose here on earth. All the rest is just small potatoes. The rest is just stuff and filler.

Being kind will bring you connection. To your spouse. To your children. To your co-workers, and friends, and acquaintances, and even to strangers. And human beings need connection. And this world needs more kind people. We have so many powerful people. And successful people. And wealthy people. But we need more kind people. I believe this world would be a whole different place if there were more truly kind people. And don't get me wrong. There are a lot of kind people out there. But we need more. And I fully intend on being one of them.

There are dozens of opportunities every day to be kind to others. Certainly at our jobs and while out running errands, with coworkers and bosses and customers and community members, we have countless opportunities to just be kind with our normal every-day encounters. But we also have instances where we have "run-ins" or interactions with other people that normally may just push our buttons. Where it may be perfectly "normal" or understandable if you act angry, or defensive, or rude. Those are circumstances where we have to be really conscious, and awake, and realize that we get to CHOOSE how we react. Those are opportunities for us to take a deep breath, pause, and choose a kinder response. And then, life also gives us plenty of areas to go out of our way to be kind. There are so many organizations that need volunteers. So volunteer! Offer to help at animal shelters, delivering meals, reading to children, singing with nursing home patients—whatever you find fulfilling and can make some time for. And I love the idea of doing random acts of kindness. Anonymous, random acts. Where the reward is not public accolades or anyone else acknowledging us for these acts. But the reward is that amazing feeling inside of you that recognizes you just made the world a little bit better by that act of kindness. Here are some ideas for random acts of kindness to try sometime, just for the great feeling it gives you:

Pay for the person behind you when you are in a drive through (I know you have both done this in the past—and that is so awesome!).

Leave a thank you note under the windshield wiper of a vehicle with Veteran plates. A note that says "Thank you for your service" and recognizes their sacrifice for our country.

Send a big box of chocolates to the nurses at a hospital with a note that acknowledges their hard work and dedication to helping people heal.

Leave a bunch of quarters with a nice note in a laundromat. "If you find this, it was meant for you. Do a couple of loads of laundry for free today, and have an amazing day!"

Send an anonymous letter to the local elementary school, thanking the teachers for helping to shape the lives and give positive influence to the kids in their care.

Those are just a few of the many random acts that can seriously change a person's day, and give them a smile and some hope, not to mention how it makes you feel inside. I challenge you to think of other things, and quietly go about doing these acts of kindness throughout your lives.

So my beautiful daughters--stay kind. You are kind right now. You were kind children, and you have turned into kind young adults. I pray that you always choose kindness. It will never steer you in the wrong direction—I promise.

Chapter 6

Don't Get Too Hung Up On Material Things

YOU'VE HEARD THE old saying "Money can't buy happiness." And on some level we all kind of believe that, but we also realize that money can buy a lot of really cool things that certainly seem to contribute to our happiness. But there are tons of research studies and tons of cases that show us that the old saying is pretty true. They did a study where they took hundreds of people who won the lottery, and hundreds of people that became paraplegics, and they had them answer a bunch of questions that measured their happiness. And of course at first the lottery winners were much, much happier than the paraplegics. But I'm sure you can guess at the results in 5 years. Five years later, the two groups measured exactly the same on the happiness scale. Those that won millions of dollars had the same amount of happiness as those that lost the use of their legs and were permanently in a wheelchair! Doesn't that just blow your mind? They didn't just take one lottery winner, and compare him to the rare, happy paraplegic. This was hundreds of people. All with the same results. That kind of blew my mind.

And there are numerous studies out there about countries and their "happiness factors." And research supports the fact that "richer" countries have more depression. Once our basic needs are met...food, water, shelter, etc...then more stuff, more money, does not necessarily correlate to more happiness.

Now that is not to say that there is anything wrong with making money, having nice stuff, or being considered "wealthy." I think that is all just wonderful! But the whole issue of money has a lot more to do with your mindset than your bank account. There are very wealthy people that are simply not happy. Maybe they are paranoid of losing their money, or are constantly stressed about making more money, or protecting their money, or are still just not satisfied with their lives. And there are also wealthy people that are very happy. Not only are they thankful for their abundance, but they are generous, and not concerned about losing their money, and beyond satisfied with their lives. On the other side of the coin... there are many "poor" people who are very unhappy. They are frustrated, and see only their lack, and feel the deep desire to have money but not be able to get it. There are also plenty of "poor" people who are very happy. They are content with what they have. They are grateful for what they do have, and seem to be unconcerned with getting more.

So you see….money is not the deciding factor. Mindset is the deciding factor. And I truly believe that money does not lead to happiness, but happiness certainly CAN lead to more money. And as backward as this seems to be, I believe that giving can certainly lead to more money. If I am feeling stressed about money, or the lack of it, I have found that the very best thing I can do is give some away. Seems crazy, but I have found it to be true. But the ATTITUDE about giving has to be right. If I give some away, but am pissy about the whole thing, that will NOT bring happiness, and will not bring more money into my life. But if I give with love, and feel good about the giving, it ALWAYS brings me more happiness, and actually brings more money into my life. It is crazy how that works, but it truly does work.

Which brings us back to the title of this chapter— don't get too hung up on material things. Stuff is just stuff. No matter if it has a designer label on it or not. We came into this earthly life with no material things, and we will leave this earthly life with no material things. It certainly can be a lot of fun to HAVE the material things while here on earth, but they are all just temporary things. There are many people out there that trade so much of their good qualities in pursuit of material things. People lie, and cheat, and sneak, and do a whole variety of mean and wrong things in pursuit of money and material things. SO not worth it.

I like to think about it like this. It is not my money. It is the Universe's money. Some of it will flow into my life, and some of it will flow out of my life. This money will enter my life, and allow me to trade it for what I want in this life. It is up to me to really evaluate just how important it is for me to use the Universe's money for what I want. But the money, and the material things I buy, are not really mine. They are here for me temporarily, just like my time on this earth is temporary, so I do not have to stress about it. I know it will flow into my life and out of my life. I do not ever have to feel lack. I can always feel the abundance of the Universe's money and that which is working its way into my life. I need to be smart with the money that comes into my life. I need to balance living for today with saving for my future, but I do not have to stress about it. I hope that no matter what you girls do for a living, no matter who you marry or make a life with, no matter how much money comes into your life or flows out of your life, that you will always focus on the abundance in your life, and not stress about money or material things.

One of the tricks I do is to count my blessings when I am paying bills. Monthly bill-paying can be really stressful for a lot of people. "Will there be enough?" "I can't believe how expensive this is!" "I'm not putting enough money into savings." (Remember that feelings are caused by thoughts, right?) So these thoughts can lead to so much focus on lack, and stress, and anxiety. So when I sit down to pay my bills, this is what I think: I pay the mortgage and think "Thank you, God, for this comfy house that we live in. Where we are safe, and protected, and where we make memories." And when I pay the utility bills, I think "Thank you so much for our heat, and our air conditioning. We are warm and toasty in here when it is cold outside, and nice and cool when the outdoor temperature is so hot." Same for the car payment.

"Thank you, Universe, for my car. I can get to and from my work, the store, go on trips, run errands, etc. My car is such a convenience, and I am so thankful for it!" Now that's some powerful thinking right there. It comes from a place of abundance, not a place of lack. And it makes paying my bills down-right enjoyable☺

Now…some practical advice. <u>Saving</u> now can make a HUGE difference in <u>having</u> later. You will spend what you make. If you make $40,000 per year, you will spend it. If you make $500,000 per year, you will spend it. So my advice is this. Right away, your very first job, start putting the maximum amount you can into retirement, especially if your company has a matching benefit. If right away you take some of your money and invest it, the rest will be your income, and you will spend it. If you don't invest any of it, that will be your income and you will spend it. Does that make sense? The bottom line is…. don't wait. Don't think to yourself that you will invest in retirement later. Because it gets harder and harder to do it, and then you feel like you are really sacrificing to have to do it down the road. If you do it from the get-go, it will just be part of the deal and it won't seem like a sacrifice. Do it your very first "real" job, your very first paycheck.

If you are paying your bills, and putting some money toward retirement, and putting a little bit in savings, and even have a little money for some fun once in awhile, well….you are doing pretty darned well. I try to live off of 55% of my monthly income, meaning that is what I use to pay my regular bills—housing, car, food, utilities, etc. Then 10% goes to retirement, 10% to savings (for planned bigger purchases or travel), 10% goes to "fun money" (for eating out, movies, happy hour, etc.), 5% goes to some type of education (online classes, guitar lessons, self-help books and courses, etc.), 5% goes towards an "emergency fund" (for unexpected car repairs, appliances that die, the surprise crown needed on your tooth, etc.), and 5% goes to charities and donations. That is roughly where my monthly income goes. And that creates an environment where I am living for today, meeting my survival needs, planning on some fun and bigger purchases, and saving for my retirement. And I am giving toward causes that I believe in. It feels very balanced, and very do-able, and I am in constant gratitude for the money that is flowing into and out of my life.

Chapter 7

The Law Of Attraction And Karma

I LEARNED ABOUT THE Law of Attraction later in life, but I've known about Karma all my life. My mom used to say "What comes around goes around." She was talking about Karma. I've truly always believed that it is that overlying "checks and balance" system. Let's say you do something a little shady, but no other human being knows about it. You can think you "got away with it." BUT…..there's karma. Karma says that it really doesn't matter that no other human being knows. Karma knows. And that shady thing will come back to you—somehow. And that is just another reason to be kind. To do the right thing. To go the extra mile to help someone out. I believe it will come back to you.

The Law of Attraction is kind of a newer concept for me, but I am really loving it. Basically, it says that THOUGHT is a vibration, and you send it out into the Universe, and it comes back to you. It is the "thinking" equivalent to the "action" of Karma. It says that when we think, we send out vibrations into the world, and those thoughts are like magnets. They attract what is like them. But even more than the thoughts themselves, it is the feeling of the thoughts that cause the vibration. I know this all seems a little weird, a little "out there", but stay with me here. This Law says that what we put our attention on, and what we feel with strong emotion, is what we are attracting into our lives. So if I am worrying, stressing, focusing on things that can go wrong….you will attract that. If you are focusing on your lack, you are drawing in more lack. BUT, if you focus on abundance, and feeling positive, and feeling really good about it all…THAT is what you are attracting. It's a pretty deep subject, and I am really learning more and more about it. I will not try to explain it any further, but I will recommend some great books about it. The first is "The Secret" by Rhonda Byrne. It is a great introduction to the subject. If you want to go a little deeper into it, "The Law of Attraction" by Esther and Jerry Hicks. They are both books that introduced the subject to me. It's all pretty fascinating. And I think that it is a Universal Law, just like the law of gravity, and it doesn't matter if you believe it or not. You can NOT believe in gravity, but here you are walking on the earth. And you can NOT believe in the Law of Attraction, but here you are drawing things into your life. And if you don't know about this law, you will be attracting things by default.

Sometimes unwanted things. So as I am learning more and more about this law, I am learning to use it in my favor. So I'd love for you girls to learn more about it and use it in your favor!

Chapter 8

Worry, Stress, And Anxiety

O K.....SO GOING BACK to the idea that your thoughts create your feelings, I want to talk about worry, stress, and anxiety. I think a lot of people just assume that worry is an essential part of life—we SHOULD be worried about all of the things that can go wrong. But I want you to realize that worry is created from what you are thinking. Period. And I really feel like it is a very USELESS emotion—but that it is common, and something we all deal with. What does worry add to the world? What does worry do for you personally? Worry is about you thinking that something negative is going to happen. It is you running bad scenarios in your mind. And truthfully, the vast majority of the time, those bad scenarios never happen. It's the "what if?" "What if I fail? What if I don't make enough money? What if I embarrass myself?" And by worrying about it, it can keep us from taking action. It can be a very damaging emotion.

But just saying "you shouldn't worry…" doesn't make it easy to stop worrying. It is a skill set to stop worrying. Number one, it's about trusting the Universe. It's about adopting the attitude that things work out exactly how they are meant to work out. Number two, it's about thinking positive. It's about training your mind to think about just how good circumstances CAN turn out, then expecting them to turn out well. Number three, it's about being willing to feel any emotion. It's about being willing to feel embarrassed, or feel left out, or feel disappointed. If you are willing to feel these emotions, you can stop worrying about feeling them. And then you can remind yourself that feelings come from what you think. So you don't HAVE to think the thought, "I'm so embarrassed. I just failed and everyone knows it." You can CHOOSE to think, "Well that didn't turn out the way I had planned. But here's what I learned from it….". These are skills that get stronger over time, the more you use them.

Stress can come from truly being overextended—biting off more than you can chew. But it can also just be sort of "made up." What I mean by that, is that we can sometimes increase the stress in our lives on our own. How? It's getting to be a theme….but it is coming from your thoughts. If you are thinking stressed out thoughts, "I'll never get this done on time." "I have too much to do." "I'm going to fail at this." Well….of course you are going to be stressed out. Stress can be debilitating, or stress can be motivating. It can make you put it in gear and get things done. But there are countless studies out there about what stress does to your body long term. And it's not good. So first of all, if you truly have too much on your plate, try to prioritize and drop a few things out. And work on your mind—what you are telling yourself. Meditate. Breathe. Make lists. Go for a walk or run. Get a massage. But do what you need to do to get your stress level down. Your body will thank you for it as you age😊.

Anxiety seems to be more prevalent all the time. Maybe it's just that in the past, people didn't talk about their anxiety. Nowadays, it seems everyone tells everyone about their anxiety. So maybe it just seems more prevalent. But regardless, I still believe that at the root of the anxiety, is the thoughts that we think. I am not a therapist, or a counselor, or even a great source on this subject, because I have never really suffered from chronic anxiety, the way some people do. But I have certainly felt anxiety, like all humans on earth do at some point. And it's a yucky feeling. So it's just natural to try to push it away. Resist that anxiety, avoid that anxiety, try to cover that anxiety up with something else. I'm convinced that those actions only serve to make the anxiety grow. And grow. And grow. The last time I felt anxiety, I decided to just feel it. This is going to sound a little weird. But I just closed my eyes and acknowledged the anxiety. I began to describe it. I had a hollow feeling in my stomach. My shoulders and neck felt really tight and tense. The back of my throat felt tingly and dry. Temperature? It felt sort of hot in my head and neck, but cold in my stomach. Color? Ice blue. Was it moving or stationary? It felt very stationary—sitting there like heaviness in my body. Rating? On a scale of 1 to 10, it felt like a solid 8. I did NOT like this feeling! But I just sat with it. And felt it. I kept telling myself, "This is anxiety. This is anxiety." And I didn't try to push it away. And pretty soon I felt my shoulders relax a little. And the heavy, hollow, stationary feeling in my stomach started to move a little bit—to get more fluid, and a little lighter. And I just stayed with it. And pretty soon, it felt like a 3 out of 10. And I thought to myself, "Well that's not so bad. I just felt a lot of anxiety, but it didn't kill me." And at the end of the 10 or 15 minutes or however long I did all of this, I opened my eyes and realized that I had moved through it. I'd come out on the other side of it. And I didn't feel really anxious anymore. And I cannot tell you how much it helped.

So....to wrap up this chapter. Worry, stress, and anxiety are common. They are emotions that we all feel. And feeling them doesn't mean something has gone wrong. But learning to "deal" with them is a huge part of managing your mental health. They can become crippling feelings that govern our lives. Or they can just be a part of life that come and go, and we learn to manage them, and they are just several of the emotions that we experience as human beings walking this earth. That's all.

Chapter 9

The Art Of Listening

*Y*OU HAVE BOTH given me examples of people that are not good listeners. Friends that are not really hearing what you are saying, and constantly go back to the subject of them and what is important to them. Annoying, right? But learning to be a good listener is a skill. It is practicing really hearing what a person is saying, without your mind drifting off. It is staying present to hear them, and not forming your response. It is being curious about what they are telling you, and not thinking of a story to tell them as soon as you can get a chance to interrupt. And that is not to say that a conversation isn't a two-way street. Of course people go back and forth with stories, memories, facts, etc. But when the other person is talking, it really is an art to just be present and LISTEN.

People love to be remembered. So when you meet a person, repeat his/her name, and make a mental note of it. When you see him again and say "Hi Brad" it really makes a person feel good. When you bump into a person you have met in the past, remember her name, and make a point to say Hi or wave or acknowledge her in some way, it may make all the difference in her day. And it goes right back to being kind. There are so many people out there that feel invisible. Do your part to make people feel good. They may not remember your name, or details about you, but they will always remember the way you made them feel.

Practice being a good listener. When your friend or family member--or even a stranger--is telling a story, really listen to her. Try to stop your mind from drifting off to your own story. Ask questions. Be truly inquisitive and curious about what she is telling you. And try, really try, not to give advice if it is not asked for. This one is tough, I know. There is just a natural tendency for us to want to put our 2 cents into everyone's life. If someone point blank asks you for advice, certainly feel free to offer your opinion. But often, a person is telling you a story, or complaining, or venting, and really not wanting you to "fix it" for them. They are just venting. So just hold your tongue and listen. It is such a valuable skill, and you can learn so much in life by just keeping your ears open.

Once again, this is one of those things that sounds easy, but can actually be difficult. Our minds are just built to think and think and think. That's what they are for! But developing some control over your mind, and being able to quiet the mind—make it slow down and settle down and pay attention to just one thing—that's an exercise that needs to happen over and over and over. That's why I like meditation. That's what "being present" is about. And that's also the skill of listening. Being able to focus your mind ONLY on what a person is saying, and nothing else. It's a valuable skill. And actually kind of rare. So work on developing it. When someone tells me, "You're such a good listener", I feel like that is a huge compliment. There are lots of people running around out there without feeling listened to. If you can listen, and not judge, and just give a person your undivided attention, that can be such a gift—to you both!

Chapter 10

The Peaks And Valleys Of Life

HAVE BEEN PRETTY darned broke in my life—really stretching the ends to meet. I have had periods where I had plenty of money in the bank. I have had times where I've enjoyed lots of friends and a very busy social life. I have had periods of being alone and feeling pretty isolated. I have had jobs that I hate, and jobs that I love. I have been heavy, and I have been thin. I have gone through moments of hating myself and my life, and periods of loving myself and my life. These are the peaks and valleys of life. And they are normal. Life is full of ups and downs. But that's what makes life on this earth pretty darned amazing. It's easy to think that we want the world to be awesome all the time, and we want to feel happy all the time. But....do we really? Do you want to be happy at a funeral? Do you want to feel great when your loved one goes through a tough time? There are just times during our lives that are going to be a bummer. That's life. You WILL experience loss. You WILL make mistakes. You WILL fail. You WILL go through rough patches. That doesn't mean anything has gone wrong. It's all just part of life.

If you can just acknowledge this as you are going through the valleys, and know that it is part of it, and know that eventually it will end and you will start to climb up to a peak again....then it makes it all much more bearable. And you will learn something from all the bad stuff. And you will get a little stronger. And you will be able to have more sympathy and empathy when someone else goes through the same thing. And it will make you a better person.

There are people that can get so lost in the bad. They will go through a rough patch, and think that they will never get out of it. They will look at all of the tough circumstances and dive into the negative thinking, so things get worse, and their thinking becomes more and more negative, and the spiral downward just continues. But if you can somehow just KNOW, deep in your heart, that everything is temporary, and that you WILL be ok, eventually, it will help you get through those rough patches. You don't have to jump onto the spiraling downhill slide. If you can just ride out the valleys, knowing it is all part of life, then you won't have to go so far down into deep, deep valleys, or stay for long periods of time in seemingly endless valleys. If you can wrap your mind around the fact that life just contains peaks and valleys, and although the valleys are not fun, they are part of life, then you will be able to have more shallow, shorter valleys in life.

And when the peaks come, then you can just really enjoy the heck out of them! There can be gratitude in your heart for this wonderful time you are experiencing. You will know, too, that the peaks—like the valleys--are temporary, so you can just soak up those beautiful times in your life and appreciate them and savor them. When I am going through a particularly wonderful time in my life, when things are just going so well, and I feel like I am just flowing and in rhythm with the Universe, I just sincerely thank God, and my Angels, and the Universe, and I allow myself to really enjoy it. When I was younger, I used to almost worry when things were going super great in my life. I would feel like "the big crash" was just around the corner. Things were going "too well", so I wouldn't let myself enjoy it all. What a waste! Now I know that peaks and valleys are all temporary. And I strive to minimize the valleys, and maximize the peaks, and do the best I can to keep telling myself that it is all normal! It is all just part of life. And what I have found as I have aged (and become so much wiser☺), is that the landscape of my life has changed. It used to be full of very steep, deep, wide valleys, and just little hills. But now, its full of high, majestic mountains, and just little dips. And I like that landscape a whole lot better! And it is ME—all ME—that gets to shape that landscape. Because I get to choose how to react to the circumstances and events that happen in my life. I get to choose to get through the valleys with hope and patience and self-love; and I get to choose to allow my heart to swell and expand and be so grateful through the peaks.

Chapter 11

The Instruction Book
We Write For Others

*W*E EXPECT PEOPLE to act a certain way. And so many times, we don't even bother to tell them what we expect of them. We write this manual for them, and then they don't follow it, and then we are mad. Sounds a little crazy, but that is what we do.

On a larger scale, there is sort of an instruction book that society writes. And that is good. It is made up of laws and rules, so that there is some sort of order in our world. The speed limit is 25mph through town to keep people safe. You drive 40, and you're going to get a speeding ticket. You can't steal other people's stuff. You can't hit people. You can't cheat. These are all part of the big manual that helps us all live together as humans. That's not what I'm talking about.

I'm talking about when you expect your friend to realize you are in a bad mood and try to cheer you up.

And she doesn't. Then you're mad at her. Or when you expect your boyfriend to know that he should plan more romantic nights for the two of you. And he doesn't. So you're mad at him. We tend to write these manuals for the close people in our lives, and the manual spells out exactly how that person should act. Sometimes we tell them how they should act, but sometimes we don't even tell that person about the manual, and then when he or she doesn't follow that manual, we are mad.

There is a book by Don Miguel Ruiz called "The Four Agreements." One of the agreements is "Don't make assumptions." That's huge. There are so many times that we make assumptions about what another person's motive is for doing the things he or she does. We make it MEAN something. An example: You see a friend at a party, and she barely acknowledges you. She says Hi, but makes no effort to come talk to you or be friendly to you in any way. You immediately start making assumptions. "She must not really like me." "She's not a very nice person." "She thinks she's so cool that she can't be seen hanging out with me." All KINDS of crazy assumptions, right? But in reality, she and her boyfriend just had a big fight, and she is really distracted, and it has absolutely NOTHING to do with you. You just made an assumption. We do this quite a bit, and SO MANY disagreements and arguments come from it.

So I have this advice for you. First—throw away the manuals. Let that person just be exactly who he or she is. Now….that's not to say that you can't ASK for a person to do something. You can tell your friend that you had a bad day, and would she please try to cheer you up? You can tell your boyfriend that you would love to have a romantic night—planned by him, and would he please do that for you? BUT…..don't hang your happiness on whether that person does it or not. I think that there is this opinion out there that when you are in a friendship or relationship with someone, that person has a responsibility to meet your needs. And trust me on this, no one can always meet your needs. That person will eventually fall short, and things will go south. But if we realize that WE are responsible for OUR OWN NEEDS, and that other people are not responsible for making us feel a certain way, I just think it makes for better relationships. And don't assume you know what another person is thinking, or why they are acting a certain way. Ask! Get the facts. I cannot tell you how many times in my life I was just making an assumption about how another person was feeling, but once we talked, I found out I was completely wrong about it all. And it sure would have saved a lot of tears and hurt feelings and drama if I just would've asked in the first place.

And realize this truth—you CANNOT change another person. Consider how hard it is to change yourself, and realize the futility in trying to change others. Life gets so much easier when you just allow other people to be who they are. There will be people that drive you crazy. That is life. You will have roommates that drive you nuts. You will have boyfriends that make you grit your teeth. You will have coworkers that know how to push your buttons. And you will have family members that drive you to the brink of insanity. That's ok. You don't have to love everyone all the time. But the minute you start to try to change him, to try to get him to act a different way, to try to manipulate how he behaves, that is where trouble starts. It is hard to do, but if you can just be fascinated by how another human behaves, just be curious about it, and observe it, and allow it, without trying to make it be any different, then these relationships can be very real. Now, that doesn't mean you have to choose to stay. You can choose to NOT be around that person. You can choose to remove yourself from the situation. But you don't have to do it with anger, or frustration, or even sadness. You can simply tell yourself that you are allowing that person to be negative and complain and be kind of nasty and bitchy, but you just don't choose to spend your time with her. And go do your own thing. This is such a hard concept to grasp—I know. But I can tell you from years and years of experience, that trying to get another person to follow your manual and behave how you want him to behave will be much harder on you in the long run.

Chapter 12

Personal Boundaries

*N*OW, I THINK its important at this point to differentiate between the Instruction Book and Boundaries. They are very different. Boundaries are something we create to take care of and protect OURSELVES. They are not created for other people. Boundaries are just kind of there—unspoken—unless they are broken. Then they have to be talked about. So let's say you have a boss that yells at you. If you make a mistake, he actually yells. This is where you have to set a very clear boundary to protect and care for yourself. You have to be clear that you do not want to be yelled at, and there should be a very clear consequence—something YOU will do, if that boundary is broken. "If you yell at me, I will walk out of your office." And then you follow through. You walk out of his office when he yells at you. And if it keeps happening, you let him know that if he continues to yell at you, you will speak to HR about it.

You are setting boundaries to take care of yourself in this example. It's different than the instruction book you write for others. Do you see the difference? One is to try to change another person, one is to protect yourself. It's a fine line, but important that you distinguish between the two.

The idea of personal boundaries has been widely written about in all kinds of self-help books. Boundaries that are too "soft" or too "rigid" can actually be part of some types of mental illness. It's a super deep subject, and I'm not going to say too much in this chapter about it. I just wanted a short little blip in here about differentiating these two things. Again, with one, you are trying to control how another person behaves. With the other, you are protecting yourself. Having a hidden instruction manual for other people can lead to lots of frustration and drama. Having solid boundaries for how other people treat you is actually a form of self-love and self-respect.

Chapter 13

Learning How To Fail

*T*HERE ARE LITERALLY hundreds and hundreds of examples of very successful people that used their "failures" to help them along in life. Thomas Edison said, "No, I didn't fail a thousand times. I learned a thousand things that didn't work." When you hear the saying, "If at first you don't succeed, try, try again," that really SOUNDS good, but it is pretty difficult to put into practice. And the reason that "failing" is so darned hard, is because of the thoughts that we think about it, leading to certain feelings. We have thoughts that make us feel embarrassed, that make us feel worthless, that make us feel disappointed. And those are not good feelings. So we in turn think that failing is not good. But I suggest reframing the thoughts that are causing those feelings. So let me take a very personal example from my life—an issue that is still something I "fail" at regularly. Losing weight. I have struggled with my weight all my life, and I could not even begin to list all of the diets that I have tried over my lifetime. Well, I am still overweight, so I guess you could say that all of my attempts in the past to lose weight have been failures. And my go-to thoughts when I "go off the wagon" and "cheat" on a diet, are thoughts that completely beat myself up. "I knew I couldn't do it—I always fail." "I am destined to be fat all of my life." "Who cares? I'll just keep eating everything in sight and get fatter and fatter." I have literally done this over and over and over since I was a little kid. It has only been recently, through all of this "mind management" stuff I've been learning, that I am trying to change all of this. In the last 6 months, I have started and stopped several "diets" or "life-style changes", whatever you want to call it. But instead of allowing those old negative thoughts to come in and make me feel like crap about myself, I've been examining the "why" behind what makes me go back to my old eating or non-exercising habits, and treat myself with love and compassion. I am trying to understand what it was about eating that way, or doing that particular exercise regimen, that just didn't work for me. I've been trying to pull out the aspects that I liked, that were easy for me, that made sense to me; and also being very honest about the aspects that just didn't fit with my schedule, or my wants, or my needs at the time. I take what I learn from it, then just decide to move on. And I am really learning so much about myself. I know it will take some time, but I've decided that the more I learn from these quote/unquote failures, the more I can take with me forward, and slowly work on something that will actually work for me long-term. And here's the best part—I'm not in a big hurry. This whole process of learning and discovering and correcting my course of action—well...that's what life is made of. And I am slowly learning to enjoy the process.

Failure is really just something that didn't turn out the way you expected. That's it. That really is not a big deal. Things sometimes just don't turn out the way we expect them to. So if you can think about it like that, and decide to learn what you can from the situation, make the changes you need to make, and just try it again, all of the sudden--failure is not such a terrible thing.

And I know it sounds a little weird, but sometimes I kind of plan ahead for failure. I tell myself that I am going out there, and trying to do this thing, and there is for sure a good chance that I will fail at it. Possibly over and over and over. But when I fail, I will have my own back. I will treat myself with respect and be proud of myself for trying, and I WILL NOT beat myself up for it. And I will plan to learn from it. I will plan for the possibility that it may very well NOT work the first time, but that I will gain a ton of knowledge from my attempt, and use that knowledge to move forward.

Failure is just a natural part of life--<u>IF</u> you actually try new things. People that never fail are people that just play it safe, never try anything new, never set new goals, never try to expand. And I don't know about you, but that just doesn't sound like a fun life to me. I think that growing, and changing, and evolving is just a really fun way to live. But it for sure involves some failure. It involves things not quite turning out the way you thought they would. It involves setting a goal and not reaching it. That's just part of the deal. But try to teach yourself how NOT to be afraid to fail. Work on your thoughts on this subject. Try to look at your "failure" as a learning opportunity. Take the lesson, adjust, and try again. And if need be, try again. And again. And again.

I think a huge part of this failure business, is fearing failure BECAUSE OF WHAT OTHER PEOPLE WILL THINK ABOUT YOU. I know that we all love to say "I don't care what other people think." But honestly, that is one of the hardest things in the world to actually overcome. We are people that exist in societies, and we deeply want approval from others. Whether that is conscious or subconscious—it is there. Millions and millions of people in this world decide to do things, or NOT do things, because of what they think other people will think of them.

Well….here's my 2 cents on that. Other people are going to judge you no matter what you do. If you take that new job, they'll judge you for being in way over your head. And if you don't take the job, they'll judge you for not being ambitious enough. If you have a serious boyfriend, they'll judge you for not being able to be by yourself. And if you're single, they'll judge you for not being able to find a boyfriend. You'll get judged if you wear that new outfit, or if you wear sweatpants. If you gain weight or if you lose weight. People will judge you, no matter what! So, why not just ignore all the judging, all of what you THINK people are thinking about you, and just do what you truly want to do? There is such an amazing freedom in this! When you can actually just allow people to think ANYTHING they want about you, and not let it influence your decisions, it frees you up to just follow your own heart, and do what makes YOU happy. I've come to a place in my life where I am just perfectly fine with people judging me and believing anything they want to about me—even if it's wrong. I can just let people be wrong about me, and still happily go on with my life. So that sets me free to try new things. To pursue new dreams. To expand my comfort zone and set challenges for myself. And if I fail—who CARES what others think of it! My work is in managing what I think of it. My work is in learning to be OK with failure, and make it mean that "it is a work in progress", not a devastating loss that I have to feel bad about.

There are people out there in the world doing things that maybe you'd like to try. And I guarantee, some of those people are less qualified and less talented than you are at those things. But those people decided to believe in themselves, learn from their failures, and not give a rip what other people think of them. So I am encouraging you girls to do just that. Do not be scared of failure. I'm not talking about being reckless, but I am talking about getting out there and chasing your dreams. Failure can crush you and make you give up, or can shape you and help you grow. You get to decide.

Chapter 14

Life Is A Journey

I KNEW YOU GUYS would laugh at the title of this chapter. But I don't care—it really is true. In life, you will always be working TOWARD something. At first, you were working towards learning to read. Then working to get through a tough high school class. Then working toward high school graduation. Now you are working on your college degrees. As soon as you have those, you will work on your career. Chances are you may get married, and work on your marriage, and then starting a family, and then getting your kids through school, etc. etc. etc. I am still working toward all kinds of goals and plans I have for myself. The point is, life is just a series of journeys working towards something. But…..so many of us think that we will only be happy, or fulfilled, or successful, when we get there--when we actually reach that destination we have in our mind. But remember, as soon as we reach that particular outcome, we start setting our sites on the next outcome. So we have to truly realize, that the JOURNEY toward these things is what makes up our lives. The day in, day out, sometimes mundane actions we take every day while we are working towards something. That is life. And it is so easy to just let that stuff slip past us, and not even realize that life is passing us by.

We've all done this—you take a drive, start off on your destination, then when you get there, you realize you have no recollection of actually driving there. You don't remember going past that one farmhouse that you usually notice, or turning at that one corner where you have to turn. You just show up at your destination, and realize your mind was somewhere entirely different, and you don't remember the drive at all. It's weird, right? Well, for so many people, life can be like that. You wake up one day, and you have a house, and a husband, and kids, and a career, and a job, and you think, "Now, how did I get here?" Your mind has been dwelling in the past, or constantly worrying about the future, and life has just slipped right on by.

So my words of wisdom here, are to stop and reflect OFTEN. Stop, really notice the journey you are on. Regularly take some time to take notice of where you are in life, realize that you are working towards something, but also realize that you don't have to be in a big hurry to get there. And that just taking stock of today, and where you are today, and who you are with, and how you are thinking, and how you are feeling, and just acknowledging the journey—right now, today—will help life to slow down a bit, and help you see the beauty that IS this journey of life.

And I'll let you in on a little secret. The journey of life is supposed to be FUN! Make no mistake, some crappy stuff will happen, but overall, we were put on this earth to live these lives and to find joy. To be happy. To have fun. To truly ENJOY the journey! So laugh at me if you must. Roll your eyes. But learn that happiness is NOT found only in the destination. Learn that getting to the destination—the actual journey—is where happiness can be found every day. If you can stop, actually bend down, put your nose in the flower, and LITERALLY—not just figuratively—smell the roses, you can live life more fully, more aware, and more appreciatively. Life IS a journey, my dear daughters. Enjoy the heck out of it!!!

Chapter 15

Gratitude

*A*ND THE NUMBER one way to enjoy the journey of life? Be grateful for it! (See chapter 3). Now, don't get me wrong. I really believe that it is perfectly fine to throw a pity party for yourself at times. Life really is full of some disappointing, sad stuff, and you have every right to sulk, feel sorry for yourself, and feel sad. So go for it—feel those feelings. But those should be the temporary, passing feelings. If the most prevalent feeling in your life is one of gratitude—true, blue, deep appreciation for your life and everything in it—then your life will be pretty amazing!

These are words that you will hear from so many religions, so many influential people from the past, and there are thousands of books written about being grateful. But if you don't practice gratitude, then it is just words. Gratitude is a skill. And skills need practice, over and over and over again, to really develop into something that is automatic and easy. So you really do need to put the work into being grateful. You have to stop, and count your blessings. You have to pray and tell God every day what you are thankful for. Keeping a gratitude journal is a really great way to make sure you are doing this every day. Write 3-5 things in a notebook every day that you are thankful for. When we really stop and think about all of the amazing material things, people, opportunities, relationships, etc. that make up our lives, there is always SO much to be grateful for. And because of the Law of Attraction (see chapter 7), the more you have the vibration of gratitude, the more things will come into your life to be grateful for. It's a win-win!!!

I love the book "The Magic" by Rhonda Byrne. Each chapter is an exercise to develop gratitude. It has you take action every day to cultivate this amazing emotion. It's easy to SAY you are grateful, but I think the magic happens when you actually take steps to BE grateful. Even if you have a crappy day—try, try, try to say 2 or 3 things that you are grateful for before you go to sleep. And when your alarm goes off, before your feet hit the ground, say again 2-3 things that you are grateful for. Make this part of your routine. I have countless blessings in my life. I know that intuitively. But to say them out loud (or in my head), makes those blessing become more real, and allows that amazing feeling of gratitude to wash through my body. I think it is one of the best feelings in the world!

Chapter 16

Working Hard

*L*IFE IS ALL about balance. It really is. You need to live for RIGHT NOW, but balance that out with planning for the future. You have to work hard, but you have to balance that with relaxing. You have to get out there and be with people, but balance that with time alone. You have to give a lot of yourself to your job someday, but that has to be balanced with your life outside of work. Life is just a balancing act. But one thing is for sure—you will feel much better about the playful, fun parts of life, and really feel like you deserve this—if when you work, you work hard. And it really doesn't matter what the job is. We can be talking about a paid employment, or chores around the house, or helping a friend with a project. When you buckle down, roll up your sleeves, and just work hard, it just makes you feel better about yourself. We all inherently know when we are slacking, or being lazy, or just not giving our best. And it makes you feel ashamed, and it lowers your self-esteem. And if you do it too much, and it becomes a matter of habit for you, it just gets easier and easier to slide by with minimum effort. But that is SO damaging to your own inner sense of pride.

There are going to be jobs, and chores, and projects, that you just do NOT want to do. You will hate the very idea of going to that job, or tackling that chore, or starting that project. But if you can just tell yourself, with your thoughts, that no matter how much you don't WANT to do it, you are GOING to do it, and you are going to do it WELL—to the BEST of your ability, then you will get through it. And you will come out on the other side of it feeling proud of yourself. And that is a great feeling.

I'm not saying that life is supposed to be hard. There are those that put so much importance and priority in hard work, that they forget that life is supposed to be fun. Again, it's about balance. But working hard builds your confidence like nothing else. When you realize that you CAN do hard things, you CAN work hard, you start to build a relationship of trust with yourself. And don't forget to acknowledge your hard work. It's ok to stop and pat yourself on the back sometimes. I'm not talking about blowing your own horn at other people, or being cocky. That's you thinking you're better than someone else. I'm talking about you having confidence. That's you thinking you are better today than you were yesterday. You should be proud of yourself when you work hard and achieve something. But don't beat yourself up when you look back and realize that you didn't work as hard as you could have. Reflect on it, learn from it, try again tomorrow. Sometimes it's just a matter of jumping in and doing it, even though you know it's going to be hard. We've all had those things that we are dreading—writing that paper. Raking the leaves. Organizing your closet. But then we jump in and just get going with it. And momentum builds. And we find ourselves working hard and just getting it done. And at the end of it, when you are maybe exhausted and maybe sore and maybe mentally fried, you also have this great feeling of accomplishment, and the knowledge that you worked hard today. And that's a pretty good feeling.

Chapter 17

Forgiveness

THERE ARE VOLUMES and volumes of books out there on this subject. It's a tough subject. Some people have a much harder time forgiving others. Some people find it easy. But know this—not forgiving someone really only hurts YOU. "Holding onto anger is like grasping a hot coal with the intent of throwing it at another; you are the one who gets burned."

I think a lot of people think that forgiveness means that you are telling a person that what he or she did or didn't do was okay—that you are condoning their behavior. But that is NOT what forgiveness is. It really is just about letting go of a feeling of anger or resentment that YOU have. And remember….feelings come from our thoughts. So if you are angry or resentful, it is 100% because of the thoughts that you are having about that person or that situation.

And any conversation about forgiveness has to include forgiving ourselves. So many people just cannot forgive themselves for things that they have done. They are ashamed of themselves, or angry at themselves, and they just can't let it go. But I want you to refer back to the first chapter. I talk about getting to a place that you believe your past happened EXACTLY HOW IT WAS SUPPOSED TO. If you can get to that place, then there really is nothing to forgive yourself for. That mistake you made, that decision you made, that "horrible" thing you did—well, it just brought you to where you are now, and it was supposed to happen exactly the way it happened. If you can really wrap your head around that, then it will be so much easier to forgive yourself. If you can look at the lessons learned, how that thing changed you, how it molded future decisions, and you can see the value in it—then you can more easily say "there is really nothing to forgive myself for." You can chock it up to lessons learned, vow to try not to make that mistake again, and then LET IT GO.

And once you can forgive yourself, it gets easier to forgive others. Not for THEIR sake, but for your sake. Holding on to feelings of anger and resentment about what another person did or didn't do really does not hurt them—it hurts you. If you can once again wrap your head around the fact that it happened EXACTLY THE WAY IT WAS SUPPOSED TO, then you can just let the feelings of anger and resentment go, and truly forgive that person. And you don't have to tell that person that you forgive him. And he doesn't have to apologize. And you can choose to not be with that person again. Just because you choose not to. But you can change your thoughts to ones that bring you feelings of peace, and that make YOU feel better. Forgiveness is a gift for you. No one else.

I have at times struggled with forgiveness in my life. I knew I needed to forgive someone, but I just didn't know HOW. I took this little mini online class on forgiveness once, through Mind Valley, and it helped me with the HOW. It outlined a 7 step process to go through. The first step is to identify the person or the act to forgive. The second is to create a space for it. Visualize where it happened, what they said, how it happened. Try to take the emotion out of it. Just be an observer—visualize it like you are watching a movie. The third step is to read the charges against them. Calmly, like you are in a court of law. "You cheated on me." "You said awful things about me behind my back." "You stole my wallet." Whatever it is. Fourth, allow yourself to feel the anger and the pain. Move toward those feelings. Really feel it, describe it, let it happen. Get those feelings OUT. Step five, think of what you may have learned from this event. Really try to explore any positive, silver linings that may be there. Maybe you learned to trust your intuition more, because you had a feeling he was cheating. Maybe you realized that your "friend" is not really a true friend after all, and that you are better without her in the end. Maybe you learned not to leave your wallet in your car. Just try to find some type of lesson in it all. The sixth step is to try to find some compassion for the person that hurt you. Try to think about how he or she may have been hurt in the past. Maybe his dad cheated on his mom and he is just repeating this behavior. Maybe she has terrible self-esteem and talks about you behind your back because she is not confident enough to stand up to others. Maybe that person that stole your wallet has had things stolen from him, and he is wounded, and feels like he now needs to steal from others. Who knows? But try to maybe see how they were thinking that may have made them react or act the way they did. And the last step is to try to visualize giving them a big hug. Can you love that person? Even if you choose not to have them in your life any longer? No? That's ok. You went through the steps. It is a process. So give it a day or two, and try it again. Work through the steps again. And again, if needed. And again. Forgiveness can be a process. It doesn't always work all at once. But these steps can give you some framework to at least work towards forgiveness.

Chapter 18

Making Decisions

E ALL MAKE decisions every day. Tiny decisions. Getting up out of bed in the morning is a decision. Going to class or to your job is a decision. We choose what to eat, what to wear, what to do in our free time, and when to go to bed. All day, every day, we are making decisions. The little stuff may not seem like decisions. They are habits. They are just what you do. But make no mistake, they ARE decisions. Because you could decide not to get out of bed. You could decide not to go to class or to work. But this chapter is not about those tiny, daily decisions. This is more about the big decisions. The ones that we really have to think about. The decisions that tend to make us worry and fret and maybe even lose sleep over. Those big decisions we all have to make in our lives sometimes.

The easy decisions are the ones we have really strong feelings for, one way or the other. No problem. But some of the most difficult decisions to make are the ones where we just get swallowed up in not knowing which way to go. We don't have strong feelings one way or the other. Or at least we don't think we have strong feelings about it. We are confused, and just unsure, and sometimes—that makes us avoid the decision. We put it off. But honestly, NOT deciding is also a decision, ya know?

I think there are a few thoughts that can really help with decision making. One technique that I like to use when making a big decision, is to consider that each one is going to be amazing, then decide. I have been offered two jobs. Think about Job A and imagine it being the most fulfilling job, with awesome co-workers, making great money, and just picture yourself being very happy there. Now do the same with Job B. Visualize it being just as awesome. If they were both to turn out completely perfect, does one or the other NOW have an advantage that becomes more evident? Because there are times that we think to ourselves that making one decision is going to turn out awesome. And making the other decision is going to turn out terrible. And we get so scared to make that decision, because we feel we will miss out on the one that's awesome. That can muddy the waters. So I have used this technique in the past to just assume that either decision I make will turn out amazing, and then as I visualize them both turning out that way, a definite feeling comes over me of which one I should choose. Something will just make decision A seem like a way better choice than decision B. Or, alternatively, I will run the best-case scenario and the worst-case scenario of each decision through my mind. Sometimes that will tease out the one that seems to have a distinct advantage over the other.

I have also used the good old "list the pros and cons" to help me make decisions. I think it can be valuable. I have had decisions to make in the past that seemed very overwhelming, and the act of dividing a piece of paper into 2 columns, and listing out all of the positive, great things about it on one side, and the seemingly negative, less great things about it on the other, has revealed to me a definite edge to deciding one way or the other. But a twist to that is to assign a number from one to ten to each of the entries on the lists. Because you may have a long list of cons, that really aren't THAT important to you, but they are cons nonetheless. And you may have one pro that is huge for you—something that really means a lot to you. So you can't just count up the lists on each side of the page. By assigning a number from 1-10 to each entry, you can better evaluate the things that are really important to you when making that decision.

But here's what I think is the most important thought you can have when making a decision: you have to wrap your mind around the fact that there are no wrong decisions. Whatever you decide, it will all play out the way it is supposed to. That's hard. That takes a whole lot of faith. That takes a ton of trust in the Universe and the belief that everything truly will work out just fine in the end. If you can just grasp that you will either succeed or you will learn, then you can proceed with the decision with confidence.

And once you make the decision, go all in. Don't waffle. Don't get stuck in the middle ground, where you have one foot in the yard of your new decision, but have the other foot in the yard of the other possibility you could have chosen. This is where people can shoot themselves in the foot before they even have a chance to explore their new decision. Because they are second-guessing themselves, worrying that they made the wrong decision, playing out the "what if's" in their head. No! Don't torture yourself that way. Once you make the decision, go 100% in that direction, knowing that you are going to just travel down that road and see where it takes you. Because here's the thing….you can always course-correct down the road. Once you have made the decision, and travel down the path, and you learn and realize that things were maybe not what you thought, or didn't turn out the way you thought they would, then you can make another decision down the road. That's OK. That happens to people all the time. And it doesn't mean you made a mistake, or that something went wrong, or that you can't trust yourself next time to make the "right" decision. It means that you got to experience this decision, and learn from it, and certain people came into your life because of it, and it can all just be part of the grand experience of your life. And you can CHOOSE to change it, if the decision no longer serves you. And you can always, always, have your own back for making the decision. Don't beat yourself up about it. You made the best decision you could at the time, knowing what you knew at the time, having the feelings you were having at the time. If you truly buy in to the fact that there is no wrong decision, then you can just change directions and make a different decision if you have to. No big deal.

And please remember this. NOT making a decision, simply because you are too afraid of failing, is one of those things that people have regrets about when they are on their deathbeds. Deciding NOT to go after a dream, or NOT to take a chance, purely because of fear, IS what I consider the worst-case scenario. Because not taking the risk, and always having to wonder what would have happened if you had, is a much tougher thing to face than 99% of the things you are so scared are going to happen. If you can look back and say, "Hell yes, girl. You went for it. You put it all out there and maybe it didn't turn out exactly like you thought it would, but you didn't sit on your couch and play it safe and let fear hold you back!" That may be what happens. But maybe, just maybe, you will be looking back saying, "Hell yes, girl. You went for it. You put it all out there and it turned out even more amazing than you could have ever imagined. You have made your dreams come true, and you didn't let fear hold you back!"

Chapter 19

Dream Big

SOMEWHERE DURING MY growing up years, I learned the concept of "Don't get your hopes up too high." I had a belief that setting my sights too high would just lead to disappointment if it didn't work out. That it is better to shoot low and not worry about setbacks than to shoot too high and suffer from defeat. What a bunch of crap! What kind of warped thinking is that? It's a very common way to think, and honestly, it's a belief I held a lot of my life. It comes from being scared of emotions. It comes from thinking that your feelings come from circumstances and other people. Once I learned that my emotions come from my thoughts, and that it's perfectly fine to feel "negative" emotions like disappointment, this whole concept of "don't dream too big" just crumbled.

I am at a place in my life where I am SO willing to dream big. Incredibly big. Even impossibly big! Because

I have now learned that I get to CHOOSE how to feel if something doesn't work out. If that huge dream does not come true—so what? I get to choose to think about it in a way that will cause gripping disappointment, or I get to choose to think about it as an adventure worth taking, no matter what the outcome. My thoughts about the situation will create my feelings about the situation. Period. End of story. And I get to choose my thoughts.

And if it doesn't pan out, and that big dream doesn't come true, maybe I WILL be disappointed. But again—so what? I can feel disappointment and survive. Disappointment won't kill me. I can feel disappointment and not let it ruin me. It's just part of the deal. I can choose to feel disappointed about it and know that it is perfectly OK to feel that way. And although disappointment doesn't feel great, it's a feeling I am willing to feel.

That frees me up to dream big—but not get attached to the outcome. And it frees me up to take risks. And it is exciting, and adventurous, and such an awesome thing to feel as if the journey towards the dream, not the dream itself, is the exciting, adventurous part. And if I'm not super attached to the outcome, but can still just have my big dreams, well….what a fun way to live!

But here's the rub. I 100% want you girls to feel like you can dream big dreams. I don't want you to buy into the "don't get your hopes up too high" mentality. But I also want you to be perfectly content with a so-called "ordinary" life, if that's your dream. If the quote/ unquote normal life, of marriage, and jobs, and kids, and backyard barbecue's, and basketball games on the weekends, and yearly family vacations, and going to the drive-in during the summer, and building a snowman in the winter, and all of those seemingly ordinary things IS your big dream—that is awesome! Be great with that! Be truly content and grateful with building a life like that. Be good at that. Work hard at that. And if your big dream is starting your own business, or planning a crazy trip to Africa, or taking off on a dream year with you and your family living in a 5th wheel camper traveling around the U.S.—do it! Don't let fear hold you back.

Be willing to really examine what lights you on fire, then be willing to go for it. And don't be scared to dream. Don't be scared of disappointment. We only get to be walking on this earth for a certain number of years (this time around☺). And we have no idea how many years that will be. So LIVE. Really LIVE.

Remember that your perspective on things is what makes your reality.

Know that your thoughts create your feelings, and you get to choose your thoughts.

Believe that there is a Higher Power that is the ultimate Source for all you need.

Love yourself—unconditionally. Be your own best friend.

Treat others with kindness.

Don't get too hung up on material things and money.

Know that your thoughts are attracting like things into your life. Know that doing good brings good into your life.

Learn to manage worry, stress, and anxiety, so they are just SMALL parts of life, not gigantic parts.

Really listen to people when they speak.

Ride through the valleys of life and minimize them if possible, and celebrate the peaks of life and maximize them all you can.

Throw away the imaginary instruction book you have for others, and just let people be who they are.

Set healthy boundaries for yourself.

Learn to fail, and make it a learning experience, not a devastating experience. And try to allow others to think about you whatever they want to—make choices in life for YOU, not for what other people will think about it.

Life is a magnificent journey—enjoy it. Don't just wait for the destination to arrive to applaud. Soak up the road that gets you there.

Practice gratitude regularly. Truly count your blessings—wake up saying thank you, go to bed saying thank you, and be grateful for all of the little things that add up to make life so amazing.

Work hard when you need to. Give it your all. But remember to balance hard work with play!

Forgive others. Realize that forgiveness is a gift you give yourself, and be unwilling to hold a grudge that only hurts you in the long run.

Make decisions with the belief that there is no wrong decision. You will rock it out, or you will learn from it, and both are just fine.

Don't be scared to dream big. Your life will be exactly as YOU design it. The possibilities are limitless—so don't let fear hold you back.

I love you so much, Zoe and Halle. You bring so much joy into my life. I hope you find some of these words of wisdom helpful in your life. I think we can only really "get" things when they are meant to be "gotten." So you may read this book today and find one particular chapter really helpful, and the others just don't really resonate. Then you may put it away in a drawer and forget about it. But maybe next year you'll pick it up, read it again, and read something that has a whole different feeling for you because of what you are going through at the time. And then maybe in five years you'll pick it up again, and a chapter that you didn't even remember now will hit different, and give you some advice you need. That is my hope, anyway. As I wrote every chapter, you girls were right there on my mind, as if I were speaking to you. I wrote this book for you, with the hope that you will get some of these concepts WAY before I did. You are both amazing young women, and way ahead of the place I was when I was your age. I am so proud of you both, and I know deep in my heart you will both have really good lives. I am deeply grateful for you both. I am a better woman because of you both.

Post-Script

A S I AM finishing this book, I am now 53 years old. I breezed through 52, made it to the other side (although we did go through a world pandemic during my 52nd year on earth!). But I lived to tell about it. And I have to say that so much of what I wrote in this book, what I now believe, was a long, long time in the making. I was 50 years old when I learned so many of these concepts. I mean, I had this inkling inside of me, I guess, about some of it. But I didn't raise you girls with some of these principles and beliefs, because I simply didn't know about them. When I was 50, I found myself pretty darned unhappy, and dissatisfied, and I knew that I had to figure out how to find happiness. I somehow knew that happiness could not be found "out there", but honestly didn't know how to begin to find it inside of me. I started by turning off the TV. I had been in the habit of watching the news every morning, and knew that it often had me feeling depressed and sullen before I even got into the shower. It set a really bad tone for my day. Then I set about the idea of surrounding myself with positivity. I searched for books on self-help and positive thinking, and those books led to podcasts on self-love and forgiveness, and that led to Instagram accounts full of positive affirmations and spirituality. And one thing just led to another, and that led me to somewhat of an "awakening." I have to give kudos to Melissa Oatman's online course "Love Your Life." That was such a great place to start my journey. Brooke Castillo and The Life Coach School Podcast truly changed my life. So many of the concepts in this book came from listening to her podcast, starting with episode #1, and listening to all of them—over 350 weekly episodes. I mentioned the books "The Secret" and "The Magic" by Rhonda Byrne. Recently, I read "The Greatest Secret" by her as well, and it has really shifted my awareness. Another amazing book is "Conversations With God", by Donald Neale Walsh. That book just resonated with me so much, and it made me find a deep peace with my spirituality. Mind Valley is an online education platform, led by Vishen Lakhiani, and is chock full of amazing education about mind, body, spirit and work. It requires a membership to have access to all of the courses, but they also offer individual classes and have a podcast. There are many others. Once I started this journey, I literally devoured all I could on these subjects. I truly have learned more in the last 3 years than I have learned the whole 50 years before them. And the best part—I feel I am only seeing the tip of the iceberg! I know that I have so much more to learn, and I am just soaking it all up like a gigantic sponge. I haven't been this excited about life for years and years and years.

I mention the above references because they really helped me, but I realize everyone has their own path. I know you will find your inspiration for life exactly where you are supposed to find it. It's so important to actually WORK on this "stuff." We tend to think there are just not enough hours in the day. But I guarantee, if you have time to scroll through Tik Tok for hours (I'm guilty of this!), watch the news and complain about the state of the world, and tune into countless television shows that are about depressing subjects….well, then you have time to read some inspiring books, listen to uplifting podcasts, be still and calm and meditate, and make lists in your head or on paper of all the things you are grateful for. We, as human beings, get to choose how to spend our time on this earth. And I hope that at least SOME of the time, you sweet girls will spend some of your minutes working on self growth and self evolution. It is part of caring for yourself, and I want you to know that you are deserving, amazing people that should care about yourselves. All human beings are. And some will get that, and thrive on this earth. So off you go….go live awesome lives☺!

Printed in the United States
by Baker & Taylor Publisher Services